Speedy Drones

Marie-Therese Miller

Lerner Publications ◆ Minneapolis

Lightning Bolt

To the aerospace engineers in our family, Erin and Ryan

Lerner Publications Company
An imprint of Lerner Publishing Group, Inc.
241 First Avenue North
Minneapolis, MN 55401 USA

For reading levels and more information, look up this title at www.lernerbooks.com.

Main body text set in Billy Infant Regular. Typeface provided by SparkType.

Library of Congress Cataloging-in-Publication Data

Names: Miller, Marie-Therese, author.
Title: Speedy drones / Marie-Therese Miller.
Description: Minneapolis : Lerner Publications, [2025] | Series: Lightning bolt books ® - mighty military vehicles | Includes bibliographical references and index. | Audience: Ages 6-9 | Audience: Grades 2-3 | Summary: "How does the military search for missing people in dangerous areas? They get help from drones. Readers will enjoy learning about the many types of military drones and the technology that make these machines work"— Provided by publisher.
Identifiers: LCCN 2023035581 (print) | LCCN 2023035582 (ebook) | ISBN 9798765626108 (library binding) | ISBN 9798765628997 (paperback) | ISBN 9798765635285 (epub)
Subjects: LCSH: Uninhabited combat aerial vehicles—United States—Juvenile literature. | Drone aircraft—United States—Juvenile literature.
Classification: LCC UG1242.D7 M55 2025 (print) | LCC UG1242.D7 (ebook) | DDC 623.74/69—dc23/eng/20230803

LC record available at https://lccn.loc.gov/2023035581
LC ebook record available at https://lccn.loc.gov/2023035582

Manufactured in the United States of America
1-1009902-51944-9/27/2023

Table of Contents

What Are UAVs?

A Reaper roars in from high in the sky. It lands on an empty highway. The aircraft doesn't have any people on board. A pilot has landed it from far away.

The Reaper is an unmanned aerial vehicle (UAV). It is also called a drone.

All branches of the US military use UAVs. Some carry weapons. They find and attack targets. UAVs can also help during natural disasters and in search and rescue missions.

Sailors set up a small drone after a typhoon.

Big UAVs

The Reaper is a big UAV. Its wingspan is 66 feet (20 m) long. It has landing gear. Landing gear has wheels that drop down during landing and takeoff.

The Reaper is controlled remotely. The pilot's instructions are sent through space satellites to tell the drone where to fly.

Satellites orbit Earth in space.

A pilot uses a computer to practice flying a drone.

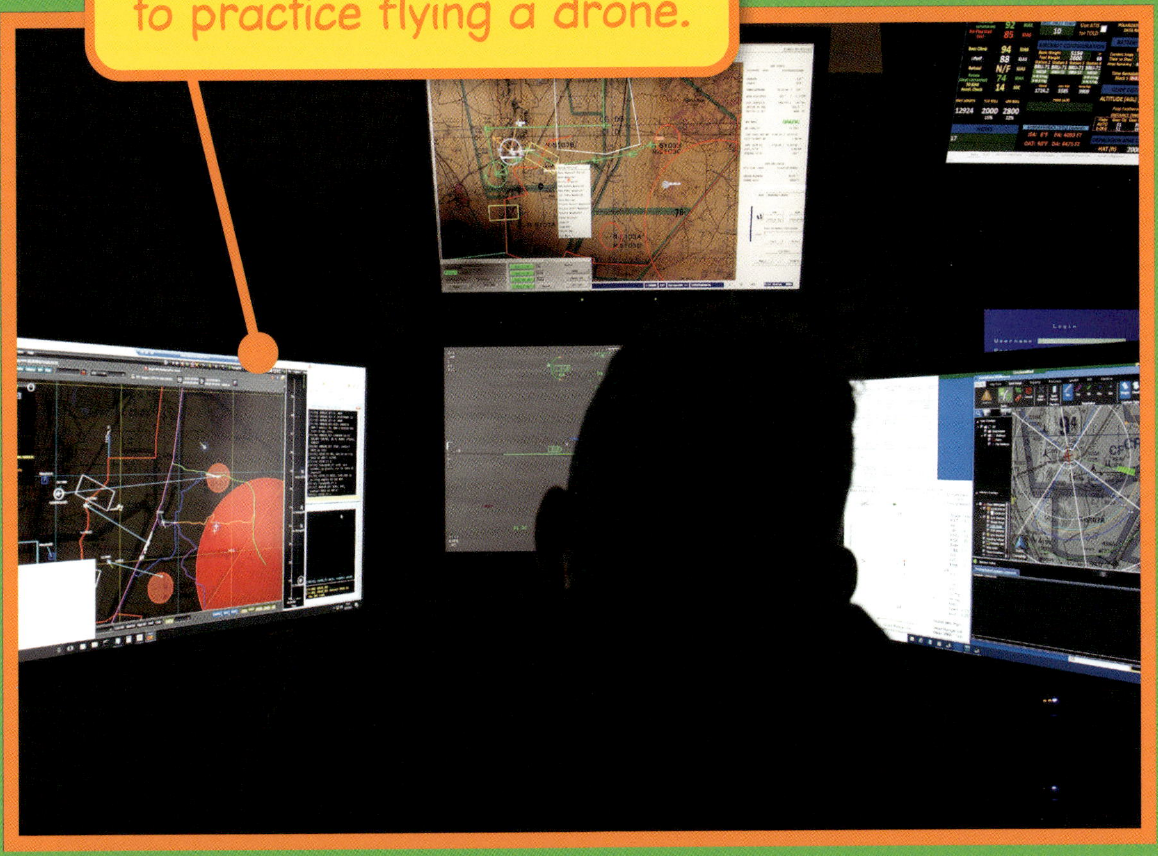

The Reaper also has autopilot. This uses computers to let it fly without a pilot. A crew member works the sensors and controls the missiles and bombs on board.

The Global Hawk is the biggest UAV in the US military. It also has wings that stay in place. It has a wingspan of 131 feet (40 m).

The Global Hawk can fly as fast as 310 knots (357 miles or 574 km per hour).

An airman prepares the Global Hawk for takeoff.

The Global Hawk has a jet engine and landing gear. It does not carry weapons. It uses cameras and radar to find people or equipment on the ground.

The navy's Fire Scout is a helicopter UAV. It has special wings called blades that spin. It can take off straight up from a ship or the ground.

A Fire Scout taking off from a US Navy ship

A Fire Scout's cameras are on the ball turret, a part on the front of the aircraft.

The Fire Scout has cameras to see what's happening around it.

Small UAVs

The US military has UAVs that are small enough to fit in a service member's backpack.

The Raven is one of these. It weighs less than 5 pounds (2.2 kg). That is lighter than a gallon of milk.

The Raven is often used for scouting in combat. Scouting is a dangerous job for people to do.

A soldier launches a Raven drone from the ground.

The Puma is also very small. It weighs 15 pounds (7 kg). Marines can use the Puma to find missing service members where it isn't safe for pilots to fly.

The military has plans to give more jobs to UAVs in the future. The UAVs could search for and rescue injured service members during a battle.

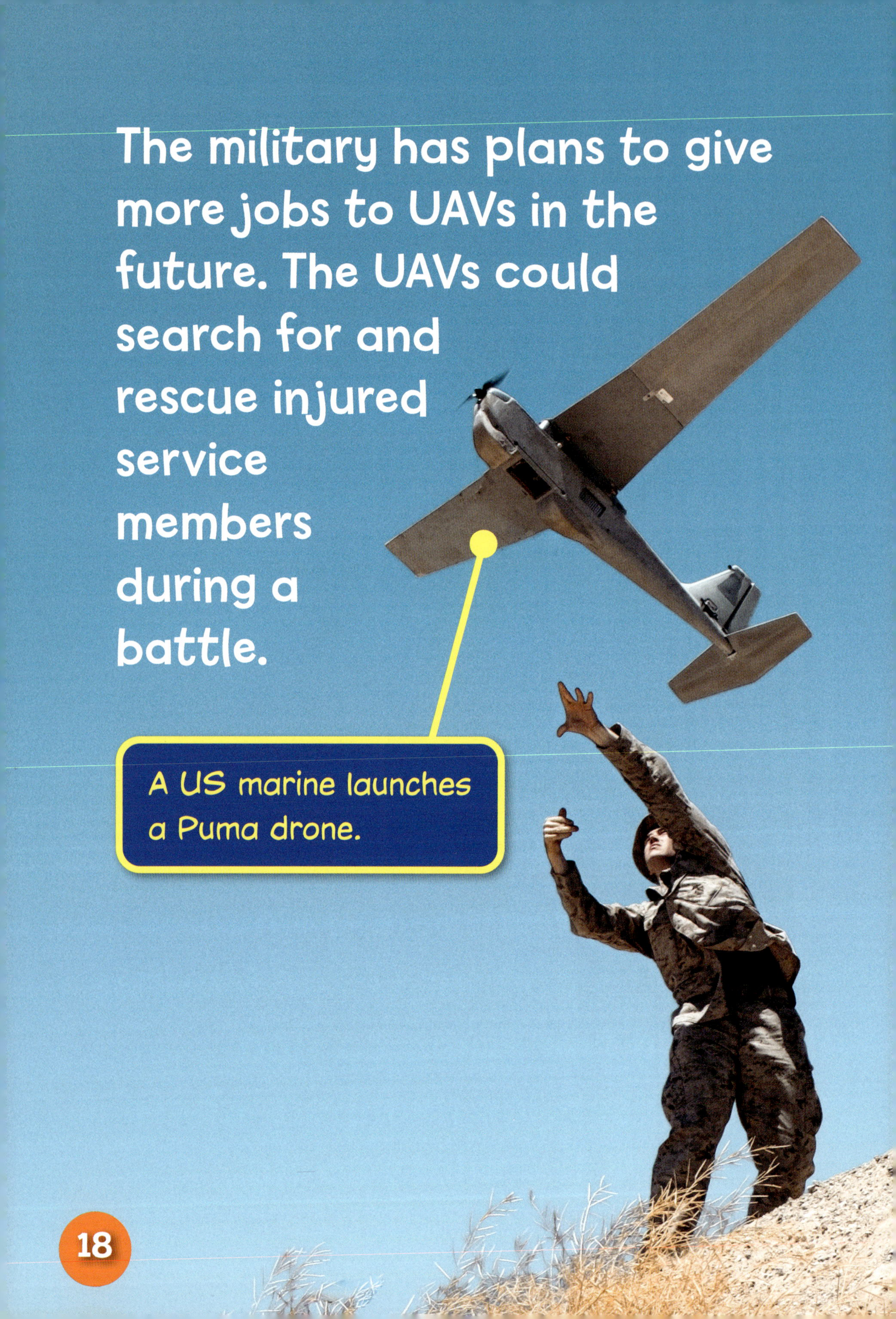

A US marine launches a Puma drone.

A Reaper parked on an air force base taxiway

Some UAVs might deliver medical supplies to the front lines. They could even refuel aircraft during flight. Drones do a lot for the military!

Drone Diagram

MQ-9 Reaper

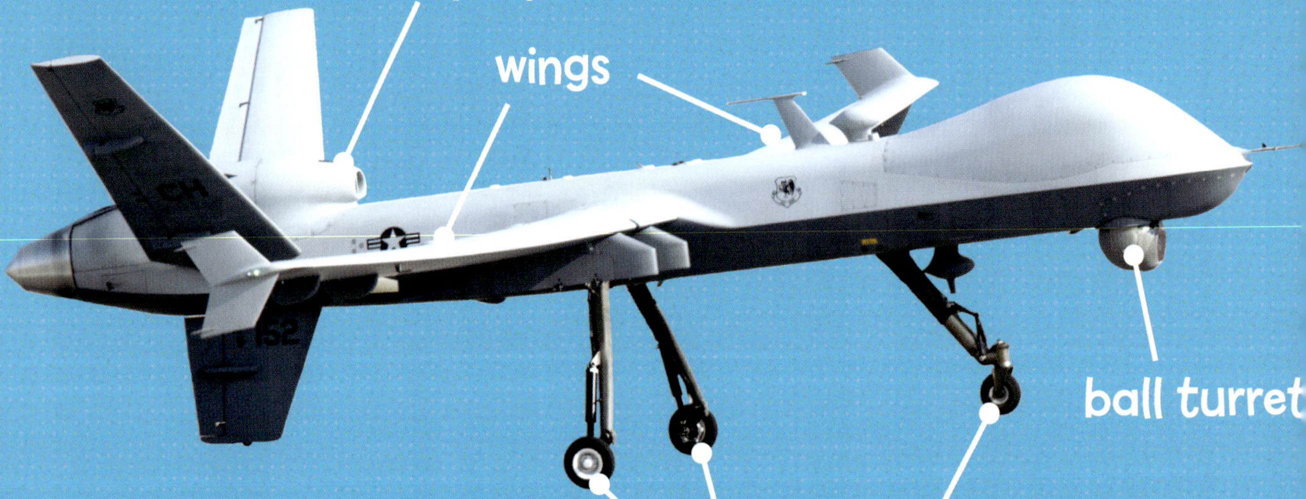

Fun Facts

- The Reaper is armed with four missiles and two 500-pound (227 kg) bombs.
- The Global Hawk can fly as high as 60,000 feet (18,288 m), higher than most planes.
- The Raven lands by stalling, or stopping in the air, then falls to the ground and breaks apart.
- The Puma can be launched from a service member's hand or by using a bungee cord.

Glossary

branch: a division of the military. The US military has six branches: air force, army, coast guard, marines, navy, and space force.

front line: the farthest point reached by combat units, often where combat occurs

mission: a specific task

natural disaster: a sudden and destructive event in nature, such as a hurricane, tornado, or flood

radar: a device that sends out radio waves to detect and locate an object

satellite: a machine that orbits Earth and collects and sends out information

scout: to explore an area to collect information

service member: a person who is a member of the armed forces

target: something fired at or marked for attack

unmanned: an aircraft with no people on board. Some countries are changing this term to uncrewed.

wingspan: the distance from the tip of one wing to the tip of the other in its pair

Learn More

Anthony, William. *Drones*. Minneapolis: Jump!, 2024.

Kaiser, Brianna. *Fast Fighter Jets*. Minneapolis: Lerner Publications, 2025.

Kiddle: Unmanned Aerial Vehicle Facts for Kids
https://kids.kiddle.co/Unmanned_aerial_vehicle

Kids Discover: Drones to the Rescue
https://kidsdiscover.com/teacherresources/drones-uavs-rescue/

McCarthy, Cecilia Pinto. *Military Drones*. Minneapolis: Kids Core, 2021.

Time for Kids: Lifesaving Drones
https://www.timeforkids.com/g34/lifesaving-drones/?rl=en-660

Index

Photo Acknowledgments

Image credits: U.S. Air Force/Master Sgt. Cody H. Ramirez, p. 4; U.S Air Force/Staff Sgt. Christine Groening, p. 5; U.S. Navy/Mass Communication Specialist 1st Class Justin Wolpert, p. 6; U.S. Air Force/Airman 1st Class Emily A. Kenney, p. 7; United States Government, p. 8; U.S. Air Force/Airman 1st Class Nicholas Paczkowski, p. 9; U.S. Air Force/Senior Airman Elora J. McCutcheon, pp. 10, 11; U.S. Navy/Mass Communication Specialist 2nd Class Danielle Baker, p. 12; U.S. Navy /Ens. Jalen Robinson, p. 13; U.S. Air National Guard/Tech. Sgt. Matt Hecht, p. 14; New Jersey National Guard/Mark C. Olsen, p. 15; Wisconsin National Guard/Amanda Clark, p. 16; U.S. Marine Corps/Cpl. Karlhendrix Aliten, p. 17; U.S. Marine Corps/Lance Cpl. Shane T. Beaubien, p. 18; U.S. Air Force/Senior Airman Haley Stevens, p. 19; U.S. Air Force/Tech. Sgt. Emerson Nuñez, p. 20.

Cover: U.S. Air Force/Airman 1st Class William Rio Rosado.